To Barb

Best Wishes
Enjoy the book

John Yao

A Collection of Memories

by John Yoniak

www.TenderFireBooks.com
Email: TenderFireBooks@gmail.com

"A Collection of Memories"

Copyright © 2019 by John Yoniak

Published by Tender Fire Books

All rights reserved. Printed in the United States of America. No part of this book may be used or reproduced in any manner whatsoever without written permission except in the case of brief quotations embodied in critical articles or reviews.

For information contact: TenderFireBooks@gmail.com

Quantity Sales available.
For details contact the publisher at the email address above.

Printed in the United States of America

ISBN: 13: 978-1-7326927-4-9

Title: A Collection of Memories

Library of Congress
Case #: 1-7630728081

April, 2019
101 Independence Avenue
Washington, DC 20559-6000

First Edition: May, 2019

A Collection of Memories

John Yoniak

Chapter Index

Introduction 7
Chapter 1 .... Hank Aaron 1964 9
Chapter 2 .... 1965 16
Chapter 3 .... New York Jets 1965 19
Chapter 4 .... New York Mets 1969 20
Chapter 5 .... Brooklyn Dodgers 1973 22
Chapter 6 .... Peter Fleming 1982 24
Chapter 7 .... Card Shows - 1980's 25
Chapter 8 .... David Cone - Early 90's 30
Chapter 9 .... Hall of Fame - Mid 90's 33
Chapter 10 .... Bryan Trottier 37
Chapter 11 .... Joe Carrieri 39
Chapter 12 .... Kenny Jonsson 42
Chapter 13 .... Bobby Thomson Bat 1951 47
Chapter 14 .... Celete Boyer 50
Chapter 15 .... Boxing 53
Chapter 16 .... Bert Young 56
Chapter 17 .... Dwight "Doc" Gooden 59
Chapter 18 .... Evander Holyfield 62
Chapter 19 .... Joe "Kelly" Vengroski 64
Chapter 20 .... Henry W. Yoniak - 1922-1984 65

~ Dedication ~

I ultimitely would like to thank my father, Henry W. Yoniak, for passing down to me his perservevance and outgoing personality.

-John

Acknowledgements

I'd like to express my many thanks to my wife and children for their outgoing support during my years of collecting and also for the time I spent in the writing, and processing of this book.

Many thanks to Stephanie Zuccaro, for helping to compile the written part of this book.

A special thank you to all the players who were so gracious over the years.

Finally, thank you to Kevin Horton and Tender Fire Books, for the assistance in the publication process.

- John

From The Author...

My love for sports started out as, I guess every young boy's does, when I was about 6-years-old.

To keep busy I'd pick up a stick, and a couple of rocks and hit away, at the time, baseballs and a bat were not readily available, so I had to improvise.

As more kids moved into my neighborhood, games got put together and the bats, balls, and gloves appeared. The sport of baseball was probably the most popular, as the saying goes, "Nothing is more American than, baseball and apple pie."

It was every kids dream to play in the Big League – Professional Baseball.

I grew up in Long Island NY. Like any small town in the United States, your parents would sign you up to play Little League ball and that's exactly what I did, the minute I was old enough.

The competition got tougher as you got older. My first coach recognized my arm and asked me to play third base, which was considered the hot corner because of the ultimate action that would come there from the batter.

As I progressed, I started to play shallow because you could take extra steps on the batter when he went to first base. The ball would come a lot faster- you had to always be alert. I would fill in as a pitcher but my true love was always third base. My most memorable play was when I was about twelve years old, playing in my first competitive all-star game in my home field city stadium in Glen Cove, N.Y.

My father had to work long hours and very rarely got to my games, however an African American man named Lloyd became my mentor. Lloyd was working at the stadium as a laborer.

I came up to bat with Lloyd behind the screen wishing me luck. The first pitch, I pulled foul down the left field line.

The other team's coach informed the outfield to shift across to left field. I then remembered something my father told me and I re-position my feet in the batter box. I moved my right foot to the extreme left. As the pitcher threw the ball, I connected and sent it to left center field for an inside-the-park home run. With that hit, I was hooked on the sport.

That was the hit that prompted my love of baseball.

As I got older my love of sports expanded and got me into

collecting memorabilia. The first autographs that I obtained were on a trip to New York City, with my older brother and friends that were crazy Milwaukee Braves fans, especially Hank Aaron.

I was probably about twelve years old, carrying only a memo pad and pen. I stood outside the Roosevelt Hotel where the players were coming out to board the bus to Shea Stadium. Among the players were Joe Torre, Sandy Alomar, Woody Woodward, Rico Carty, and lastly Hank Aaron.

He was told to get on the bus but chose to sign autographs for us kids. It was very kind of him, and when I saw him thirty years later I told him what he did many years earlier.

Ricky Henderson was sitting next to him and remarked that it was so nice I had remembered him for that.

As you read this book, I hope you enjoy, as I do, all my memories over the many years.

John Yoniak

Introduction

Double Day Field Cooperstown N.Y.

As a young boy growing up in the 50's and 60's, everyone loved the all American game of baseball. Being from Long Island the most popular team and everyone's favorite team was the New York Yankees. Even though Mickey Mantle was everyone's favorite, my favorite was Roger Maris. As a little league baseball player, I always played 3rd base and occasionally pitched.

I can truly say, with my love of playing the game is how

my passion for collecting began. I still have my first baseball glove from when I was a young boy. Many years later, as an adult, I had it signed by the player whose model it was – Bob Gibson. He noticed, when he saw it, that it was very flexible. I explained it was about forty years old and used for many years.

My love of the 3rd base position was talked about many years after when I spoke to All-Star 3rd baseman, such as George Brett, Mike Schmidt and my friend Clete Boyer, whom I would see on my annual trips to Cooperstown, N.Y.

Chapter 1

Hank Aaron 1964

My love for collecting autographs started young, with a few top players. On a trip to New York City with my older brother and a few friends we went to the Roosevelt Hotel.

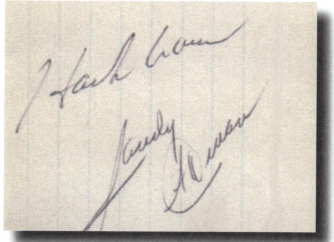

TOP SIGNATURE: *Henry Louis Aaron* *major league baseball right fielder who serves as the senior vice president of the Atlanta Braves. He played 21 seasons for the Milwaukee/Atlanta Braves in the National League (NL) and two seasons for the Milwaukee Brewers in the American League (AL), from 1954 through 1976.*
BOTTOM SIGNATURE: *Santos "Sandy" Alomar Velázquez Jr.* *professional baseball catcher, coach, and manager. He played in Major League Baseball catcher for the San Diego Padres, Cleveland Indians, Chicago White Sox, Colorado Rockies, Texas Rangers, Los Angeles Dodgers, and New York Mets between 1988 and 2007.*

As the players boarded a bus to Shea Stadium, we were able to obtain the authographs of many notables, such as Phil Niekro, Lee Thomas, Sandy Alomar, Hank Fischer, Tommy Addison, Woody Woodward, and of course that famous Joe Torre.

I also got Hank Aaron's autograph. Mr. Aaron didn't get on the bus until he signed autographs for everyone. I met up with him 25 years later in New Jersey at a show and thanked him for the autograph.

He appreciated that I remembered him. Ricky Henderson sitting nearby said that it was wonderful that I remembered and came back to thank him.

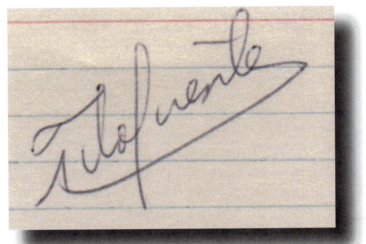

Rigoberto Fuentes Peat a retired professional baseball player. He played for 13 seasons in the major leagues between 1965 and 1978, primarily as a second baseman. Fuentes played for most of his career with the San Francisco Giants.

*TOP SIGNATURE: **James Leroy "Lee" Thomas,** as general manager of the Philadelphia Phillies from 1988 to 1997, Thomas built the Phillies from a below .500 club into the 1993 champions of the National League. In his playing days,*

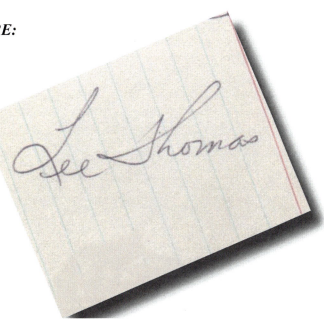

Thomas was a powerful outfielder and first baseman who batted left-handed and threw right-handed. Originally a member of the New York Yankees organization (1954–61), he was signed by Yankees scout Lou Maguolo but was later traded to the expansion Los Angeles Angels on May 8, 1961.

William Frederick "Woody" Woodward played nine seasons in Major League Baseball, primarily as a shortstop, but is better known for his tenure as general manager of the Seattle Mariners.

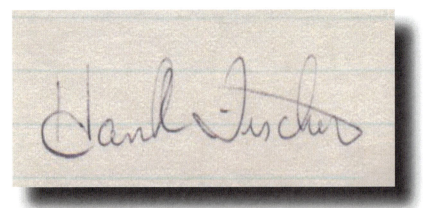

Henry William Fischer, *Major League Baseball pitcher between 1962 and 1967. Fischer was signed by the Milwaukee Braves as a free agent in 1959. He played for the Cincinnati Reds (1966) and Boston Red Sox (1966–1967) and the Braves (1964).*

John Howard "Fat Jack" Fisher former pitcher with the Baltimore Orioles, San Francisco Giants, New York Mets, Chicago White Sox and Cincinnati Reds between 1959 and 1969.

Hubert Doc Hilton, heavyweight boxer from my hometown of Glen Cove NY.

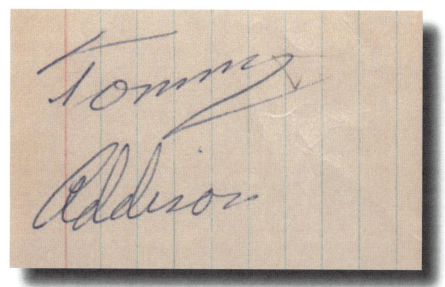

Thomas Marion Addison, was a professional football from 1960 to 1967, and is a member of the South Carolina Athletic Hall of Fame. He played his entire NFL pro career with the The New England Patriots.

Winston Hill was drafted by the Baltimore Colts football team in 1963, but signed as a free agent with New York's American Football League franchise in the same year that they became the New York Jets, and went on to record the tenth-longest string of starts in pro football history at 174.

Edward Emil Kranepool spent his entire Major League Baseball career playing for the New York Mets. He was predominantly a first baseman, but he also played in the outfield.

James Alan Bouton, was a pitcher for the New York Yankees, Seattle Pilots, Houston Astros, and Atlanta Braves between 1962 and 1978. He has also been a best-selling author, actor, activist, sportscaster and one of the creators of Big League Chew.

A Collection of Memories 15

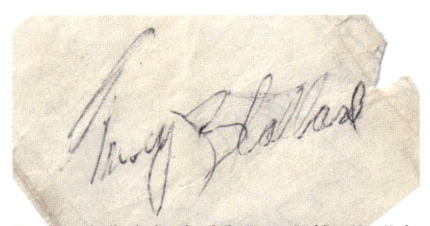

Evan Tracy Stallard, played with the Boston Red Sox, New York Mets and St. Louis Cardinals as a pitcher.
Stallard is most remembered for having given up New York Yankees slugger Roger Maris' 61st home run in 1961.

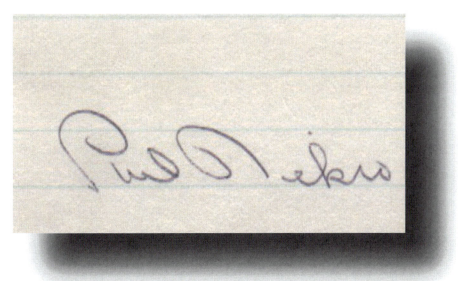

Phil Niekro, played 24 seasons in the majors, 20 of them with the Milwaukee / Atlanta Braves. Niekro's 318 career victories are the most by a knuckleball pitcher and ranks 16th on the overall all-time wins list.

Chapter 2

1965

When the baseball season was over a group of baseball greats would go out and tour schools for exhibition and fundraising and play games against the current teachers. Among the players representing Art Baumgartner's squad included Al Jackson, Dennis Ribant, Ed Kranepool, Al Downing, Jim Bouton, Joe Torre, Al Lewis, and Tracy Stallard.

One fellow in particular who played for the Glen Cove, NY faculty was boxer Hubert Hilton, once a heavyweight contender (The Happy Wanderer). Born August 18th, 1939, managed by Danny Festa and trained by Howard Davis, Sr. He fought from 1963-1978, Pro record 17-8-2. 17 KO's fought Henry Cooper, Jim Ellis, Oscar Bonavena.

Mets – Cardinals Game, August 21st, 1965 at Shea Stadium.

My father took my brother Joe and I, along with other father and sons in the neighborhood to the game. While at the game I caught a foul ball, which I wrote on "Fisher and Groat." Approximately forty-five years later, I had the ball signed in person by Jack Fisher – pitcher on the Mets, and Dick Groat – batter on the Cardinals. They were both amazed I still had the baseball.

John (l) with John Howard "Fat Jack" Fisher, a former pitcher with the Baltimore Orioles, San Francisco Giants, New York Mets, Chicago White Sox and Cincinnati Reds between 1959 and 1969.

John (r) with Dick Groat holding a foul ball that John caught August 21, 1965 and later got signed by him and Jack Fisher. Groat played for four National League teams including the Pittsburgh Pirates and St. Louis Cardinals, and was named the league's Most Valuable Player in 1960 after winning the batting title with a .325 average for the champion Pirates.

Chapter 3

New York Jets 1965

On Sunday, December 19th, 1965, my friend Harry White called me and invited me to a Jets' game at Shea. His father had a meeting in Jersey and drove us along with other classmates to the game. We sat in row V, the last row in the stadium, so high it seemed we could touch the planes headed to LaGuardia airport over head.

The weather was so cold so we spent most of the game in the bathroom for the heat. After the game was over, we stayed outside the players exit for autographs. I remember one of my classmates, Bill Gerlich, dropped his pen and Sherman Plunkett accidentally stepped on his finger.

I saved the stub from the game and had it signed by Joe Namath fifty-one years later.

Chapter 4
New York Mets 1969

I was at the game against the Astros when the Mets clinched the division series. When the game was over we all jumped over the dugout onto the field and participated in the celebration.

I now have a bat from the reunion of 1969 Mets World Champions.

John visits with the 1969 Mets Players, (l to r) Ed Charles, John and Cleon Jones

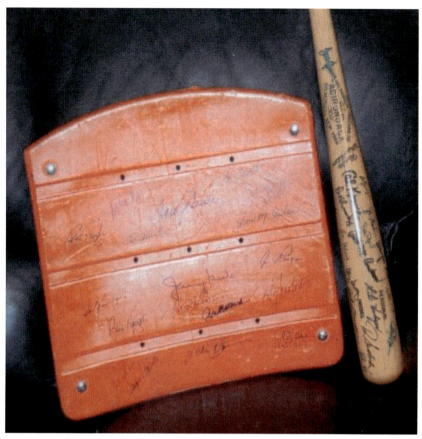

Above: John's Shea Stadium seat has 23 autographs by Mets Players. The bat is signed by the 1969 Mets including, Tom Seaver, Ed Charles and Ron Swoboda.

Shea Stadium was a stadium in Flushing Meadows–Corona Park, Queens, New York City. Built as a multi-purpose stadium, it was the home park of Major League Baseball's New York Mets for 45 seasons (1964–2008), as well as the New York Jets football team from 1964 to 1983.

The venue was named in honor of William A. Shea, the man who was most responsible for bringing National League baseball back to New York after the Dodgers and Giants left for California in 1957. It was demolished in 2009 to create additional parking for the adjacent Citi Field, the current home of the Mets. This is when John came into possession of the seat.

Chapter 5

Brooklyn Dodgers 1973

In 1973, as I was cutting lawns after work, I was introduced to a man looking for someone to cut his lawn.

I learned, after speaking to him, that he was the bullpen catcher for the Brooklyn Dodgers.

He was now working for Cove Cadillac as a salesman. He asked me if I collected boxing memorabilia. I said not yet, but that I'd appreciate anything he might have.

He told me he had a boxer coming in on Sunday to purchase a few cars and would try to get something for me.

At the beginning of the week he brought me a nice piece of memorabilia- everlast black shorts from Mohammad Ali.

Above: From John's collection, Mohammad Ali's shorts. Muhammad Ali was a leading heavyweight boxer, and he remains the only three-time lineal champion of that division. His joint records of beating 21 boxers for the world heavyweight title and winning 14 unified title bouts stood for 35 years.

Ali retired from boxing in 1981 and focused on religion and charity. In 1984, he was diagnosised with Parkinson's syndrome, which some reports attributed to his boxing career, though he and his physicians disputed that. He remained an active public figure globally, but in later years he made increasingly limited public appearances as his condition worsened. He was cared for by his family until his death on June 3, 2016.

Chapter 6

Peter Fleming 1982

One of my landscaping customers told me he was moving to Virginia and had sold his home to Peter Fleming. At the time the name didn't ring a bell with me. I later found out he was John McEnroe's doubles partner.

We struck up a good friendship for a couple of years but then he moved away. I had met John McEnroe numerous times at his house. Over the years Fleming and McEnroe gifted me a lot of Nike clothes, one of his many sponsors.

When traveling on vacation with my wife, I would always be asked where I received the clothes, they couldn't be bought in stores. When he moved, I obtained two autographed rackets by McEnroe and Fleming to add to my collection.

Chapter 7

Card Shows - 1980's

Throughout the 1980's I went to many card shows, met numerous athletes and obtained autographs. I met Joe Namath for the first time, which started our ongoing friendship. I went with my cousin Paul Deegan to Hofstra for the Jets reunion. He wanted to see Matt Snell because Paul's father worked for the Snell family in the past.

In 2017, I helped out at the Viscardi Center for the annual sports fundraiser and I got paired up with Joe Namath.

In 2013, I went to the Rock and Roll Hall of Fame

Matt Snell with John's son J.R.

Whitey Ford (r) at Cooperstown with John and his children, Krystal and J.R. Nicknamed "The Chairman of the Board," he is a former professional baseball pitcher who had his entire 16-year Major League Baseball career with the New York Yankees.

Steve Carlton with John. Carlton, nicknamed "Lefty," is a former Major League Baseball, left-handed pitcher. He pitched from 1965 to 1988 for six different teams in his career, but it is his time with the Philadelphia Phillies that he received his greatest acclaim as a professional. He won four Cy Young Awards. He was elected to the Baseball Hall of Fame in 1994.

A Collection of Memories | 27

Steven Patrick Garvey played in Major League Baseball as a first baseman, most notably for the Los Angeles Dodgers.

John (r) met with Joseph Elliott Girardi who played for the Chicago Cubs, the Colorado Rockies, the New York Yankees and the St. Louis Cardinals.

Mike Schmidt signs an autograph for John

in Cleveland with my wife. While there I went to Canton, Ohio to the Football Hall of Fame. I took pictures of Joe Namath's locker but it was lacking something. I got into a conversation with two visitors and I informed them something was missing. His fur coat was there, knee brace, white shoes, but no panty hose.

I still see Joe Namath every May, as he comes back to Long Island for a fundraiser. He loves to give back to the community.

Warren Spahan, former Milwaukee Braves pitcher, shares a laugh with John

John shows Bob Gibson of the St. Louis Cardinals an origional Bob Gibson glove which John got as his first glove.

Chapter 8

David Cone - Early 90's

I worked for David Cone (of the New York Mets) taking care of his landscapping in Cove Neck, NY. Our relationship came to a halt when he was traded to Toronto – won the World Series that year, then to Kansas City Royals and finally to the New York Yankees. Early in the year of 1996, the Yankees were having a fan festival at the Javitts Center in New York City. For a fee of $30

David Cone (l) played for a few teams including, the New York Met's, The Blue Jays, and the The Royals. On 7/18/1999 he pitched a perfect game when he played with the NY Yankees.

New York Yankees hat with signitures of former Yankee Players: Above Don Zimmer, Tommy Hendrich, Hank Bauer, Johnny Blanchard, Under the brim: David Cone, and Derek Jeter.

you had three hours to obtain as many autographs as you could. I got Don Zimmer, Johnny Blanchard, Tommy Henrich ("Old Reliable"), and David Cone. Cone had told me to see this young rookie – said he was going to be a star. I'm glad I did, because the rookie was #2, Derek Jeter.

Chapter 9

Hall of Fame - Mid 90's

I started making yearly visits to the Baseball Hall of Fame in Cooperstown in the mid 90's.

I'm still collecting induction pins to this day.

After my son was born in 1989, my dream for him was to play baseball and follow in my footsteps.

In 1995, he started with T-ball, but didn't like it because he said it was too boring just standing around.

Baseball was over for him and winter was here, so I took him to learn how to skate. I signed him up for lessons. Turns out one of the other kids in the lessons was Gunnar Esiason, Boomer Esiason's son. Right away I became friendly with Boomer who said if I needed anything signed, just ask. So of course I took him up on the offer. Shortly there-after, Boomer retired from Pro Football and became a commentator.

Speaking of Cooperstown again, on one visit there, I got to be friends with Clete Boyer. He played 3rd base with the New York Yankees. I would see him every summer and got to spend time talking about the Yankees – On occcasion, I would take him out to lunch.

I once met Pete Rose, had a bat signed and told him he should be in the Hall of Fame. He laughed and told me I should be on the committee. While standing in line with my son on a very hot day, getting closer on line to see Pete Rose, my son asked if we could get something to drink after the autograph. Pete, overheard and said, "Let me get him a drink," and bought bought J.R. a Coke.

At Cooperstown a wax figure of Casey Stengel (l) and Babe Ruth's overcoat.

Above: Reggie Jackson (l) says to John's son, J.R., "Hey you have the same hair cut as me!"

Reginald Martinez Jackson, professional baseball right fielder, played 21 seasons for the Kansas City / Oakland Athletics, Baltimore Orioles, New York Yankees, and California Angels. Jackson was inducted into the National Baseball Hall of Fame in 1993.

John's son J.R., visits with the original players of the Rockford Peaches, the team the movie League of Their Own was based on. The Rockford Peaches were a women's professional baseball team who played from 1943 through 1954 in the All-American Girls Professional Baseball League.

Chapter 10

Bryan Trottier

I traveled to Golden, Colorado in December of 1998 to visit friends for Christmas. Upon arrival I called the Pepsi Center to speak to Bryan Trottier. I had done work for him in his Manhasset (NY) home back in the 1980's. We had a short friendship because he went to Pittsburgh to play and coach. He returned the call and told me to come to the rink for one of the Colorado Avalanche practices. As I arrived at the rink I saw a familiar face. The notable person was Scott Hamilton. I got an autograph from him for my wife.

After that, I went to the security desk and they escorted my son, my daughter and I, down to the ice where we met up with Bryan Trottier, Joe Sakie, Peter Forsberg, and goalie Patrick Waa.

John Yoniak

Bryan Trottier (r) with John's daughter Krystal and son J.R. Trottier played 18 seasons in the National Hockey League (NHL) for the New York Islanders and Pittsburgh Penguins. He won four Stanley Cups with the Islanders, two with the Penguins and one as an assistant coach with the Colorado Avalanche. He holds the NHL record for points in a single period with six (four goals and two assists) in the second period against the Rangers on December 23, 1978. He is also one of only eight NHL players with multiple five-goal games.

Chapter 11

Joe Carrieri

I met Joe Carrieri at one of the baseball shows. Joe was the Yankee batboy from 1949-1955. He wrote many books about his adventures and told great stories. He said he felt lucky to be among some of the greatest Yankees including Joe DiMaggio, Yogi Berra, Mickey Mantle, Roger Maris, just to name a few.

I invited him to a local Knights of Columbus meeting where I was Grand Knight. The members loved it.

Through Joe, I was able to visit the team clubhouse where I met Mickey Rendine, manager at Yankee Stadium.

Mickey told me numerous stories about the Yankees. When the team went on the road he roomed with "Scooter" Phil Rizzuto. Mickey introduced me to Sean Landeta who punted for the NY Giants and earned two Super Bowl rings in 1986 and 1990. A fabulous guy and athlete.

Joe Carrierri, former bat boy from 1949 to 1955 for the NY Yankees shares his experience with the Knights of Columbus in Glen Cove, NY

John with Sean Landetta, former punter, NY Giants who won two superbowls 1986 and 1990
Sean was a punter who played in both the United States Football League and the National Football League. Landeta played 22 seasons in the National Football League for five different teams between 1985 and 2006. Landeta was named to the 1980's All-Decade Team as the first punter and the 1990s All-Decade Team as the second punter, as chosen by the Hall of Fame Selection Committee members.

Chapter 12

Kenny Jonsson – Swedish Hockey Player

One Sunday afternoon, after coming back from an Islander game, my wife and I stopped at our local supermarket in Glen Cove, NY to do some shopping.

There, I spotted Kenny Jonsson and his girl-friend shopping. I asked his girlfriend, who later became his wife, if she thought it would be OK to congratulate him on a good game that day. I approached him and he thanked me for my remarks.

After our meeting he started to recognize me at the many Islander functions and finally one day, he quipped, "Do you work at all?"

I laughed and said I own a landscaping business, so I was very flexible. He later asked me to take care of his house in Locust Valley and to manage it when he was in Angelholm, Sweden in the off-season.

In 2006, the Swedish Hockey team won the Olympic gold metal. Above photo show Kenny Jonsson, Sweedish defenseman with gold metal and signitures of the entire team on a jersey.

The 2006 Winter Olympics was held at the Torino Palasport Olimpico and the Torino Esposizioni in Turin, Italy. The men's competition was held from February 15 to 26 and was won by Sweden. The women's competition was held from February 11 to 20, and was won by Canada.

Hello John!

I hope that everything is good with you and your family. We are doing great. I have been busy after the Olympic gold. Lots of congratulations from people that I know and I don't know.

Here is a gift from me and team Sweden as a thank you for cheering for Sweden during Olympics in Turin 2006.

I give you a call soon.

Sincerely

Kenny

Above a letter received by John from Kenny Jonsson. Inset: Jonsson, playing badmitten with John's Son JR in Angelholm Sweeden when John and his family visited.

He married Anne Lee and they started their family with a son, named Axel. A few years later, Kenny asked me if I would play Santa and bring Axel his gifts on Christmas Day. I agreed and he lent me a Santa suit, which I dressed up in and arrived at his house with the gifts, a great memory and honor.

Anne Lee had a few of her girlfriends asking for someone to do landscaping work at their homes. I acquired Jason Blake and Chris Osgood as clients. These guys were fabulous, and would share many stories about their hockey careers. Chris Osgood had two Stanley Cups to his name when he played golie with the Detroit Red Wings.

In 2004, my family was invited to visit Kenny's family in Angelholm. Kenny recommended my son who plays hockey, to an invitational only camp in Stockholm, Sweden. After a few days we met Kenny's parents and his best friend, when he was growing up Benny.

While there, on a Friday night, in his neighborhood, one of his friends came with a cooler full of beer. He said it's happy hour around 5pm, and I felt right at home.

When we brought my son to the Swedish Hockey Institute in Stockholm, I met Ben Gustafsson – Swedish National Coach.

Kenny retired from the Islanders in 2004 but didn't stop

playing hockey. He went back to playing for Rogle, his hometown team.

I remained friendly with him and just before the Winter Olympics in 2006, I called him in Sweden to wish him good luck. He thanked me and said they would try their best. Well, they did and won the Gold Medal. Kenny sent me a Swedish jersey signed by the whole team with a hand written letter from him thanking me for cheering.

Kenny also, so kindly gave me his last Islander Jersey, his last pair of Bauer skates, a pair of game used gloves and two sticks.

Kenny was named best defenseman in the 2006 Olympics.

Chapter 13

Bobby Thomson Bat 1951

In the 1990's one of my friends informed me that his father was moving and selling his home. His grandfather had worked at the Polo grounds and had a bag full of wooden bats in the garage. He asked me if I wanted them, and of course I said yes. I identified the players as – Don Kolloway, Whitey Lockman, and Bobby Thomson. I did my research and found that Bobby Thomson used bats from the bat manufacturing company Adirondack, in 1951, these bats were made by Adirondack.

These bats were definitely game used, and they had codes on the bottom of the knob to denote what player they were from. In 1951, Thomson was famous for the home run he hit off of Ralph Branca to win pennant for the New York Giants. The Giants won the pennant with, "The shot heard round the world."

I took the bat to Cooperstown in 2001 – which was the fifty-year anniversary of that famous homer. I was told to see the curator to ask him to verify that it was the same bat as the one in the Hall of Fame exhibit. The Bobby Thomson exhibit was on the third floor. The curator checked the bottom of the knob of their bat and I in turn showed him the 146A on my baseball bat.

I was so happy to learn that, in deed, in my possession, was that same bat.

I later learned in the trade journal, that Ralph Branca and Bobby Thomson were going to be at a sports show at Freeport Rec Center.

After arriving at the show, I noticed other players from that historic year were in attendance.

I gathered autographs from Alvin Dark, Larry Jantzen (the winning pitcher from NY Giants), Bobby Thomson (who hit the historic home run), and Ralph Branca (who gave up the home run).

Seeing that it was the fiftieth year since that game, he autographed the bat and inscribed "50 year Anniversary of Shot Heard Round the World."

At Cooperstown the exhibit of the bat, glove and hat of Bobby Thomson from the famous, "Shot Heard Round the World." Below John and his son J.R. getting a bat signed by Bobby Thomson.

Chapter 14

Celete Boyer

New York Yankee's third baseman, in the late 50's to 60's, Celete Boyer, gathered five World Series rings. Since I went back to Cooperstown for a number of years, I would see Celete many

John meets with Clete Boyer, former 3rd baseman of the NY Yankees in the early 1960's.

times and after awhile, we became friends.

I told him I played third base myself, but never got to his level of play.

He told me about the wonderful years with the Yankees and that he enjoyed his expcrience, though he shared, that they never made the salaries of what the athletes make now, so they would have to get a second job in the off season.

He would hustle signing autographs, especially at the induction weekend at the Hall of Fame in July. After seeing him many times, he gave me a photo of the famous "61" in field. Bill ("Moose") Skowron, Tony Kubek, Bobby Richardson and Celete Boyer were there.

Unfortunately Celete passed away in 2007.

Above: Clete Boyer, former 3rd baseman of the NY Yankees in the early 1960's at Cooperstown induction weekend.
Bottom: John with Ernie Shavers.

Chapter 15

Boxing

While going to sports shows, I would meet numerous boxers and I enjoy the sport.

One of my most memorable encounters was when my wife and I went to Jupiters, in Franklin Square, NY. To see "Smokin' Joe Frazier Revue," which had Joe singing with an entourage of Dancers in a Las Vegas revue. After he performed I got to meet with him, he laughed when I said he should stick to boxing.

John at the International Boxing Hall of Fame at Canasota NY, standing along side the origional boxing rink from Madison Square Garden.

Above: John exchanges punches with Vito Antuofermo former Middleweight champ from 1971 to 1985. Below: John with Renaldo "Mister" Snipes, former Heavyweight contender.

Roberto Duran – Hands of Stone -Middleweight

Mark Breland – Olympic Gold Medal- Lightweight

Matthew Saad Muhammad – Contender

Earnie Shavers – Heavyweight

Renaldo "Mister" Snipes – No.1 Heavyweight contender

Howard Davis – Olympic Gold Medalist

(One of my neighbor in Glen Cove, NY)

Vito Antuofermo – Middleweight champ

If you ever get a chance, go to Canastota, NY to the International Boxing Hall of Fame do it, it's small, but very enjoyable.

Chapter 16

Bert Young

Upon arriving at a show at Nassau County Museum of Art in Roslyn, NY, I noticed a car pull up.

I immediatley reconized the passenger in the back. I called out "Yo' Paulie!"

It was Bert Young, who played Paulie in the of Rocky movies as Rocky's brother-in-law.

I told Bert I enjoyed the movies and have a bunch of items signed by Stallone. He asked me if I would want anything signed by him? Of course you know my answer.

He signed a picture I had of Rocky memorabilia displayed in my home.

John brought Burt Young a photo of his Rocky collection Including the robe from Rocky II among other items. Burt happily signed the photo.

John with The original statue of "Rocky" in Philidelphia PA.

Chapter 17

Dwight "Doc" Gooden

My niece, Tara worked for the Mets. One of her duties included escorting veteran player's around the stadium, one day she was given Doc Gooden.

Doc Gooden (l) with John, who Gooden started to call "Uncle"

I saw an ad in the paper showing that he was appearing at the Book Revue in Huntington, NY, signing his book. I arrived at the signing, listened to him talk and waited for him to sign the two books that I purchased.

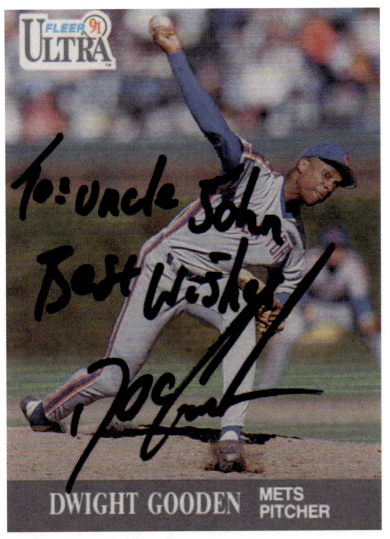

A signed baseball card from Dwight Gooden, from the mid '80's Note the, "To Uncle John."

At my turn, I asked him to personalize one book to my niece Tara, "Happy 25th Birthday." After I said her name he immediately dropped his pen, looked up and said "Tara, I know Tara."

A few days later he saw Tara and said, "Hey, I met your Uncle!"

A few weeks after that, I went to the All-Star Fan Festival at the Javitts Center in New York and was waiting in line to see John Franco when a side door opened and Doc walked in. I waved and he immediately came right toward me and said, "Uncle John! How are you?" He was there selling his books.

It didn't end there. A few months later I went to Steiner Sports to get Gary Sheffields autograph to add to my collection.

I waited in line to see Doc and Gary Sheffield for autographs and when Doc saw me he told Gary, "This is Uncle John... Uncle John this is Gary, my nephew."

Chapter 18

Evander Holyfield

It was March 2017 when I stopped by a local 7/11 store in Glen Cove, NY. One of the employees said there was a heavyweight boxer in the Italian restaurant nearby visiting friends.

As I'm a true Alabama Football fan, I had my jacket on so I thought I would stop by to see the boxer. As I walked in he noticed my jacket and shouted out to me, "Hey Bama-fan."

I turned around to see Evander Holyfield.

I had met him at a show years before and got an autograph. It was ironic that, that very morning, I was cleaning in my room at home and came across a pair of trunks signed by Mike Tyson.

If you remember, Tyson took a chunk out of Holyfield's ear during one of their matches. When I told Holyfield about the shorts he laughed and asked me if the piece of ear might still be in the shorts.

At the moment I had nothing for Holyfield to sign, but really wanted his autograph. I asked the man in the pizza shop for a

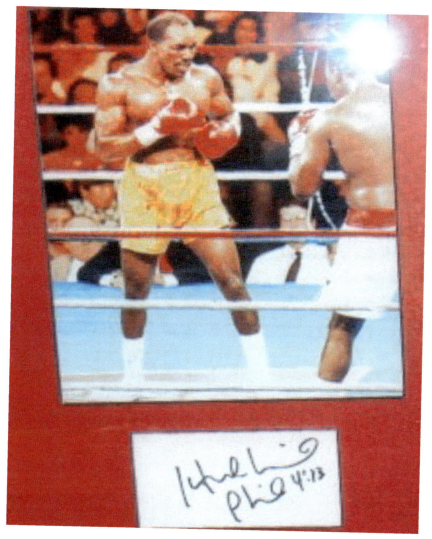
Evander Holyfield signed photo.

paper plate. Holyfield graciously signed it and told me he grew up in Alabama. He also told me that, the following September, his son would be playing football for the University of Georgia. I watched some games on TV and did see him playing.

Chapter 19

Joe "Kelly" Vengroski

While at a party at my house, my wife's Uncle Kelly viewed and enjoyed my collection. He owned a bar and restaurant, in Garden City Park called the "Garden Inn," for many years.

He said the New York Yankees would come there in the 1950's to hang out.

Sadly, when he sold the restaurant, he left most of the sports memorabilia that he received from the players in the restaurant, but he did share one iconic piece: A full newspaper that showed pictures on the back page of Yogi Berra jumping into Don Larsen's arms on the historical perfect game five of the 1956 World Series. I later got it signed by both.

Also with the newspapers, Uncle Kelly gave me the program and a ticket stub from that game. Other programs and ticket stubs he had were 1955 Brooklyn Dodgers, 1957 and 1958. Another ticket stub he gave me was from 1955 Rocky Marciano's last fightm, who retired after that, undefeated.

Chapter 20

Henry W. Yoniak - 1922-1984

Born and raised in Forest Park (Locust Valley, NY), Henry W. Yoniak, my father, grew up as the second youngest of six children.

He lost his father when he was five-years old. After graduating from grammar school he had to decide either to go to Carle Place High School or Glen Cove High School, since Locust Valley didn't have a high school of its own.

He learned to shoot baskets in his backyard with a bushel basket on hinges that would swing loosely from its mount on the outside of the house.

The make-shift hoop worked in his favor though. He was later nicknamed "Shoosh," as he never hit the rim. From 1940-1943 he played for Glen Cove high school. In those times there were no real tall men playing. The biggest man was about 6'2" and thus the center on the team. His name was Charles Sumczyk, "Shoes" was his nicknamed.

The high school was on Forest Avenue, where the Glen Cove Middle School now stands. My father told me that on Friday nights they would play for an estimated 1,500 fans.

My dad got to be captain of the team, and in 1943, they won the State Championship. They were picked to play the Harlem Globetrotters. What a thrill that must have been.

Many of the students of the time had their career cut short as WWII was going on and they were drafted into the war.

My father joined his three older brothers who were already in Europe serving. He graduated High School but his older brothers hadn't, so they were placed in the infantry. My father was in the quartermaster division, setting up the camps.

His only encounter with his older brothers was seeing them marching by the camps.

He lost his older brother, Walter, in the invasion of Normandy.

I think that if the war wasn't going on, he probably would have gone to college to play basketball and who knows what would have happened.

While in the service in the 871, he played basketball competing against other regiments and was the leading scorer numerous times from 1943-1944. In 1946, my father was discharged and came home to resume normal life.

He played semi-pro for five years and then decided to start his family.

My mother, Rose, who was his highschool sweet-heart, kept a scrapbook of all his achievements.

John's father, Henry, played in the 871st WHIPS. Right is a story which appeared in the local paper in 1943.

871ST WHIPS 872ND, 42-18

FEB. 1944

The 871st QM Fumigation and Bath company gratified a year's ambition Friday night by luring the 872d on to the basketball floor and shellacking them 42-18.

After a slow, ragged first half during which the boys from Troy and Schenectady tried to accustom their smoke-dimmed eyes to the lights of the outer world, the 871st cagers got out their brooms and swept up their old buddies like one of La Guardia's snow plows inhaling a blizzard. Yoniak was high scorer with 16 for the 871st while McGee's 7 was high for the losers.

The box score:

871st (42)

PLAYER—	FG	FT	TP
Hoffman, rf	2	0	4
Breen, rf	1	2	4
Nolan, lf	3	0	6
Brown, lf	2	0	4
Fleming, c	3	0	6
Schwartz, c	0	0	0
McClure, rg	1	0	2
Saul, rg	0	0	0
Yoniak, lg	7	2	16
Totals	19	4	42

872nd (18)

PLAYER—	FG	FT	TP
McGee, rf	3	1	7
Strockbine, c	0	0	0
Gioia, c	0	0	0
Evans, rg	3	0	6
Halufska, rg	0	0	0
Babbar, lg	0	3	3
Verbillis, lg	1	0	2
Meenan, lf	0	0	0
Totals	7	4	18

Score at half: 871st 14; 872nd 10.

Three More Nominated For Sports Hall of Fame

James "Red" Malloy

James "Red" Malloy was widely known as a mainstay on the Western Front semi-pro football team in the 1930's.

Malloy played for the team at right guard from 1932 through 1937, making the All North Shore team in 1934-35.

Malloy also served his city as a fireman for 47 years and currently lives in Glen Head.

Henry Yoniak

Henry Yoniak was captain of the 1941-42 championship basketball team and played five years of semi-pro basketball.

In the five years of semi-pro ball Yoniak played, he was considered one of the top shooters in the Northern Division. He averaged about 15 points per game in each of those five years, being chosen for the all-star team for three years.

Robert Gribbin

Robert Gribbin was captain and played center for the Glen Cove High School 1943 undefeated county championship football team. He was picked All-County and All-Metro which took in schools from the rest of the state, New Jersey and Connecticut.

He resides in Brookfield Center, Conn.

Above, story from the local paper when Henry was nominated for the Glen Cove Hall of Fame in 1987 by John Maccarone Sr.

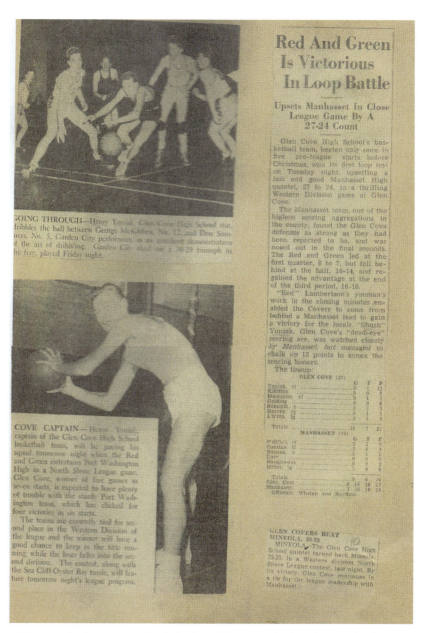

Pictured above is John's father, Henry, playing basketball in 1942-43 for Glen Cove High School.

Above: a photo John took of Joe Namath football locker at the Hall of Fame Canton OH. John later brought it to Namath and he signed the photo.

John gets an autograph from Joe Torre. From 1996 to 2007, he was the manager of the New York Yankees and guided the team to four World Series championships.

A signed Sport Illsutrated with Mohammad Ali and Smoking Joe Frazier.

A Collection of Memories | 73

Photo of Casey Stangel first Mets manager in 1962 signed by a number of Mets players from 1962 and up.

Photos From The Cover

COVER PHOTO, CENTER: John with Major League Baseball Player Gary Carter. His major league career spanned 19 seasons, most of which as a catcher for the Montreal Expos and New York Mets. He led the Mets to the 1986 World Series Championship.

In May 2011, Carter was diagnosed with four malignant tumors in his brain after experiencing headaches and forgetfulness. Doctors confirmed that he had a grade IV primary brain tumor known as glioblastoma multiforme.

Carter died on February 16, 2012, at the age of 57.

COVER PHOTO, TOP LEFT: John with James Timothy "Mudcat" Grant a former Major League Baseball pitcher who played for the Cleveland Indians (1958–64), Minnesota Twins (1964–67), Los Angeles Dodgers (1968), Montreal Expos (1969), St. Louis Cardinals (1969), Oakland Athletics (1970 and 1971) and Pittsburgh Pirates (1970–71). He was named to the 1963 and 1965 American League All-Star Teams.

In 1965, he was the first black pitcher to win 20 games in a season in the American League and the first black pitcher to win a World Series game for the American League. He pitched two complete World Series victories in 1965, hitting a three-run home run in game 6, and was named The Sporting News American League Pitcher of the Year.

John Yoniak

COVER PHOTO, TOP RIGHT: John (r) with Michael Thomas Richter, former professional ice hockey goaltender. He played his entire career with the New York Rangers organization, and led the team to the Stanley Cup in 1994. He also represented the United States in international play on several occasions. Richter was named to the U.S. Hockey Hall of Fame, alongside his former Rangers and U.S. teammate Brian Leetch in 2008.

He is widely considered to be one of the most successful American-born goaltenders of all time.

COVER PHOTO, BOTTOM RIGHT: John with Basketball player, Walter "Clyde" Frazier. As their floor general, he led the New York Knicks to the franchise's only two championships (1970 and 1973), and was inducted into the Naismith Memorial Basketball Hall of Fame in 1987.
Upon his retirement from basketball, Frazier went into broadcasting; he is currently a color commentator for telecasts of Knicks games on the MSG Network.

John Yoniak

COVER PHOTO, BOTTOM LEFT: John with Joe Namath, a.k.a. "Broadway Joe." Namath played for the New York Jets for most of his professional football career during the 1960's and '70's. He finished his career with the Los Angeles Rams. He was elected to the Pro Football Hall of Fame in 1985. He retired after playing 143 games over 13 years in the AFL and NFL, including playoffs. His teams had an overall record of 68 wins, 71 losses, and four ties, 64–64–4 in 132 starts, and 4–7 in relief. He completed 1,886 passes for 27,663 yards, threw 173 touchdowns, and had 220 interceptions, for a career passer rating of 65.5. He played for three division champions (the 1968 and 1969 AFL East Champion Jets and the 1977 NFC West Champion Rams), earned one league championship (1968 AFL Championship), and one Super Bowl victory.

Made in the USA
Middletown, DE
25 June 2019